MAKING
HEALTHY
F O O D
C H O I C E S

Do You Know Where Your Food Comes From?

Neil Morris

Designed by David Poole and Geoff Ward
Printed and bound in China by South China
Printing Company

10 09 08 07 06
10 9 8 7 6 5 4 3 2 1

**Library of Congress Cataloging-in-
Publication Data**
Morris, Neil, 1946-
  Do you know where your food comes
from? / Neil Morris.
    p. cm. -- (Making healthy food choices)
  Includes index.
  ISBN-13: 978-1-4034-8575-5 (hardback)
  ISBN-10: 1-4034-8575-5 (hardback)
  ISBN-13: 978-1-4034-8581-6 (pbk.)
  ISBN-10: 1-4034-8581-X (pbk.)
  1. Nutrition--Juvenile literature. 2. Food
industry and
trade--Juvenile
literature. I. Title. II. Series.
  RA784.M6256 2006
  363.8--dc22
                                  2006003973

Acknowledgments
The publishers would like to thank the
following for permission to reproduce
photographs:
Alamy Images p. 25 (Robert Harding); Corbis
pp. 4, 6 (Gail Mooney), 7 (Wolfgang Kaehler),
9, 11 (Henry Romero/Reuters), 18 (Bohemian
Nomad Picturemakers), Corbis 21 top, 22
(David Samuel Robbins), 23 (Pablo Corral
V), 28 (David Muench), 29 (Jeremy Horner),
30 (James L. Amos), 31 (Michelle Garrett),
33 top, 34 (Giry Daniel), 35 (Vittoriano
Rastelli), 41 (Amanda Gazidis; Ecoscene),
45 (Mark Peterson), 47 (Carl & Ann Purcell);
Getty Images pp. 12 (Stone/ Gary John
Norman), 13 (Stone/ Peter Cade), 19 (Paul
S. Howell/ Liaison), 27 (Stone), 33 bott
(Taxi/ Allan H. Shoemake), 38 (Lambert), 43
(Robert Harding), 46 (Lonely Planet/ Angus
Oborn), 49 (Image Bank/ Lambert); Harcourt
Education Ltd pp. 50 and 51 (MM Studios);
Lonely Planet Images p. 24 (Lindsay Brown);
Maria Joannou p. 40; Photolibrary p. 21 bott
(Foodpix/ Joe Pellegrini); Rex Features pp. 14
(Garo / Phanie), 37, 42 (JIAN CHEN).
Symbols on p. 10 www.transfairusa.org and
www.fairtrade.org.uk

Cover photograph of rows of eggs
reproduced with permission of Getty Images
(Image Bank/ Stephen Marks).

The publishers would like to thank Nicole
Ann Clark RD for her assistance in the
preparation of this book.

CONTENTS

Any words appearing in the text in bold, **like this**,
are explained in the glossary.

THE WORLD OF FOOD:
We Can't Live Without It

Food is one of our most important basic needs. However, do you ever wonder where your food comes from? Many of the ingredients were probably bought in your local supermarket. But where were the vegetables grown originally, and what kind of farm produced the meat? Is it local food, or has it traveled halfway across the world?

We cannot live without food. It provides us with the energy we need for everything we do. There are all sorts of foods grown in different parts of the world. This means we have a wide selection to choose from. The choices we make are important for our health, and where our food comes from might affect some of those choices.

WORLD TRADE NETWORK

In the poorer, developing countries of the world, many families farm the land and grow their own food. Others buy food from local farmers. But in the richer, more developed countries, most people depend on the food industry. They buy their food from stores and supermarkets. This is made possible by a **world trade network** in food.

▶ People of all ages can enjoy eating a family meal together. Food is a basic need, but it can also be fun.

Many countries produce more food than they need, but others do not produce enough. Those with a **surplus export** it to other countries. Exporting and **importing** countries form a world network.

In many parts of the world, **crop** farming is big business. Big companies trade the staple foods that form the basis of people's diet. These include the leading crops of wheat, rice, **sorghum**, and corn. The table below shows where the major **cereal grains** are produced and which countries export and import the most. You will see that the top producers are not always the biggest exporters. The figures depend on how much food a country needs for its own people.

Cereal grains: The world's top five producers and trading countries

grain in millions of tons per year		1st	2nd	3rd	4th	5th
barley	produced	Russia 19.8	Canada 14.3	Germany 14.3	Ukraine 12.2	France 12.1
	exported	France 6.8	Germany 3.5	Russia 3.4	Ukraine 2.1	UK 1.2
	imported	Japan 1.5	China 0.5	Belgium 1.3	Netherlands 1.3	Italy 1.0
corn	produced	U.S.A. 328.4	China 145.1	Brazil 46.3	Mexico 22	France 17.3
	exported	U.S.A. 47.4	China 18.1	Argentina 13.1	France 7.8	Hungary 1.4
	imported	Japan 18.7	South Korea 9.7	Mexico 6.4	Taiwan 5.6	Egypt 4.5
rice	produced	China 203.9	India 137.1	Indonesia 58.5	Bangladesh 41.8	Vietnam 39.1
	exported	U.S.A. 2.2	Uruguay 0.1	Argentina 0.04	India 0.03	France 0.02
	imported	Mexico 0.8	Brazil 0.8	Turkey 0.2	Costa Rica 0.2	Nicaragua 0.1
sorghum	produced	U.S.A. 12.9	Nigeria 8.9	India 7.2	Mexico 6.9	Sudan 5.7
	exported	U.S.A. 5.5	Argentina 0.8	France 0.2	China 0.1	Brazil 0.03
	imported	Mexico 3.7	Japan 1.7	Spain 0.8	Italy 0.3	Israel 0.1
wheat	produced	China 100.6	India 79.5	U.S.A. 64.9	Russia 46.5	France 43.6
	exported	U.S.A. 27.7	France 18.1	Canada 12.9	Australia 10.5	Russia 8.4
	imported	Italy 7.7	Brazil 7.3	Japan 5.7	Egypt 4.5	Spain 4.3

INTERNATIONAL CITIES

Do you live in a large town or a city? Approximately half of the world's population does, and the numbers are increasing all the time. In richer countries three out of every four people live in urban areas. It will be four in every five by 2030. In addition to moving from rural areas to cities, people are also moving from country to country.

The result is that modern cities have a variety of people. In many cities people with similar backgrounds form their own communities. Many large cities in North America and Europe have their own Chinatown, for example. Multicultural cities offer a wide range of foodstuffs so that individual communities have the option to make traditional meals.

WOW!

In New York's Chinatown, you can buy Chinese food, Thai curries, Japanese salads, Malaysian barbecue dishes, Vietnamese spring rolls, and much more.

▲ There are plenty of busy food stores and restaurants in New York's Chinatown district.

▲ Lots of different vegetables are grown on this farm in northern Tanzania. There are more than ten million small farms in this African country.

The food industry is geared toward making food cheaply so that it is affordable to buy. Many people think that healthy food is still too expensive, but is it really? If people in the developed world were prepared to pay more for their food, it would help farmers and food producers everywhere. Rich countries might also be able to afford to give more food aid to developing countries. What do you think—should developed countries pay more for their food?

Food for all?

✔ Enough food is produced all over the world for every person in the world to take in more than 2,700 calories of energy every day. This is more than enough for good health. However, many people do not have enough land to grow the food they need or enough money to buy food.

✔ At least 800 million people (12 percent of the world's population) do not have enough food to lead healthy lives. They are starving.

COMMERCIAL AGRICULTURE: ?
The World's Most Important Industry

In the developing world, most farmers produce just enough food for themselves and their families. They are called subsistence farmers. Those who manage to produce more food than they need sell the excess as cash crops.

Many subsistence farmers, especially in Africa, use the same methods that their ancestors used hundreds of years ago. They do all the work themselves and have very little machinery. But commercial farmers, and especially those in richer countries, have found new ways to increase food production. Commercial agriculture is the world's most important industry because it provides us with all our food. Modern methods involve using more and bigger machines, which are expensive. This means that large-scale farms need a lot of money to start and run.

Mechanized farms employ fewer people. Yet about half the world's workers are still employed in agriculture. This is more than in any other industry.

MIXED FARMS

Many commercial farms grow a range of crops, and many raise a variety of animals. This is called mixed farming. These farms have the advantage that they can sell a range of food to local markets and stores. If there is a problem with one of their crops—because of bad weather or disease, for example—it is not disastrous for farmers. They can still make money from other crops and animals.

In industrialized countries, many farms have become bigger, but more specialized. This is especially the case in the United States, where the vast majority of farms are specialized and often take up huge areas of land. Potato and dairy farms are good examples of specialized agriculture. About 330 million tons of potatoes are produced around the world every year, and a quarter of them are grown in China. In 2005 scientists traced the history of the first-ever potato back to Peru more than 7,000 years ago. All modern varieties are descended from this, but today Peru produces far fewer potatoes than producers such as the United States.

On specialized dairy farms, large herds of cows are kept for their milk. Dairy farming techniques have changed dramatically over the years. Cows used to be milked by hand, which took a long time and needed many farmhands. Today farmers use milking machines. This makes it more profitable for the farmer and cheaper for the consumer.

Potatoes and milk: The world's top five producers and importers

millions of tons per year		1st	2nd	3rd	4th	5th
potatoes	produced	China 82.7	Russia 40.8	India 27.6	U.S.A. 22.5	Ukraine 21.5
	imported	Netherlands 2.0	Belgium 1.1	Spain 0.8	Italy 0.7	Germany 0.7
cows' milk	produced	U.S.A. 85.5	India 41.7	Russia 34.1	Germany 30.9	France 26.0
	imported	Italy 1.5	Germany 1.3	Belgium 0.9	France 0.4	Spain 0.3

▲ Farmers in Wisconsin plow their fields according to the shapes of the land. There are many dairy, cereal, and vegetable farms in the state.

HELPING SMALL FARMERS

Like many other people, you would probably like to help farmers in poorer parts of the world. What if you were able to choose food items produced by small farmers rather than by giant food companies? Well, now you can, by looking for a Fair Trade label on the food you buy.

Millions of small farmers in the developing world find it difficult to make a decent living. They often have to sell their produce to big companies rather than directly to customers. When prices are low, they earn very little. The Fair Trade system means that they can earn a fair amount for good produce.

The Fair Trade label first appeared in Europe in 1986, when a Dutch company bought coffee directly from small suppliers in Mexico. The idea spread quickly, and now 21 countries are members of an organization called Fairtrade International.

When you see this symbol on a product, it means that it has been checked by Fairtrade International. The symbol on the top left is used in the United States. The symbol on the bottom right is used in most of Europe and Japan.

When you see this symbol, the farmers who produced the crop were paid a fair price. You may find the logo on bananas and other fruits, juices, honey, coffee, tea, chocolate, cocoa, sugar, nuts, and sometimes flowers.

▶ Chris Martin and the rest of Coldplay are ambassadors for the *Make Trade Fair* campaign. Here the band stands with farmers in a cornfield near Mexico City.

FRAGRANT HIMALAYAN RICE

India is the world's second largest producer of rice. In the northern Indian state of Uttaranchal, in the foothills of the Himalayan Mountains, small farmers specialize in growing long-grain rice. They call their rice basmati, which in the Hindi language means "fragrant," because it has a pleasant, nutty smell. In the past the Himalayan farmers sold their rice to **agents** at the local market and often received very low prices. This made it hard for them to support their families.

In 2003 a group of more than 500 growers joined the Fair Trade system. Now they receive a guaranteed price for their high-quality rice. This has made it possible for them to help other villagers build new roads and improve local schools. Fair Trade Himalayan basmati rice is sold in the United States, for example.

Many supermarkets have introduced an in-house label for Fair Trade foods (that is, a label with the supermarket's name on).

INTENSIVE FARMING

Some farmers use special methods to produce the greatest amount of crops, meat, or eggs in the shortest time and for the smallest cost. This is known as **intensive factory farming**. The advantage is that the cost savings can be passed on to the consumer. This makes food cheaper, which many people say is a good thing, especially for poorer people.

However, there are problems with intensive factory farming. One problem is that the quality of produce can drop along with the costs, especially where animals are concerned. Animals kept in conditions where they cannot move around freely are less healthy than those that lead freer lives. This usually means that the quality of their meat, milk, or eggs is not as good. Many people also think that intensive methods are cruel because animals need space, sunlight, and fresh air to lead healthy lives.

BATTERY, BARN, OR FREE-RANGE EGGS?

To produce the most and cheapest eggs, hens are kept in **battery cages**. Their eggs roll down from the cage and are caught in a trough.

WOW!

It is estimated that there are 4.7 billion egg-laying hens in the world. About 75 percent are kept in cages, but more will probably be kept indoors in the future.

▲ Many people think intensive farming using battery cages is cruel and should be banned.

Barn eggs are produced by hens that are kept in loose flocks inside barns. The birds are allowed to roam throughout the barn. Free-range hens lead more natural lives. They wander around the farm during the day and go into specially built hen houses at night.

A recent study showed that free-range eggs have more **vitamin** A and higher levels of **omega-3** fatty acids, which are good for human health. The **nutrients** in eggs are also dependent on the quality of feed given to hens. You therefore have a choice. Those from hens in battery cages may be labeled "eggs from caged hens." If the label does not say where the eggs came from, you can assume it was an intensive factory farm. Barn and free-range eggs will be labeled. They are also more expensive.

BIRD FLU PROBLEMS

IIn 2005–2006 there was a scare that migrating birds were carrying a disease called avian flu (also called bird flu) around the world. The wild birds could infect free-range hens and other farm birds, so experts advised keeping poultry indoors. This meant an increase in barn hens. Although there was no evidence that the deadly H5N1 bird-flu virus could be passed to humans by eating infected poultry, some countries began destroying farm birds and vaccinating others. Bird flu is bound to have a big effect on the free-range farming of poultry.

▼ These pigs are allowed to roam. Their meat will be sold as "free-range pork."

FISHING

Fish is a major foodstuff. Years ago fishing fleets were made up of small boats. People who lived near the coast waited for the day's catch and had a choice of fish at the market. This is still how things work in small fishing villages all over the world. Choice is limited by what happens to be caught that day.

Things are very different in other countries, though. Large fishing fleets are made up of huge **factory ships**. These vessels can travel across the world's oceans, make big catches, and even freeze the fish on board. Most of the fish in your supermarket will have been caught this way, especially the fish sold in the frozen section.

▼ These fishermen are sorting and packing their large catch of sardines.

People fish all over the world, in rivers as well as the oceans. You will find frozen fish in your supermarket, as well as canned fish such as tuna and sardines.

Some fish is also **cured** (smoked, dried, or salted). Just over half the fish caught is sold fresh, more than a quarter is frozen, and the rest is canned or cured.

Fish farming, or aquaculture, is also practiced all over the world. Fish, such as salmon, are reared in freshwater tanks and then kept in large seawater pens near the coast. Experts say that this is the fastest-growing sector of animal food production. The biggest fish-farming nations are in south and east Asia—in China, India, Indonesia, Vietnam, and Japan.

PROTEIN AND FAT

All kinds of fish contain a lot of **protein**, which is an important nutrient. High-protein meat, eggs, and fish should make up about 10 to 15 percent of our diet.

Fish are quite low in fat, but oily fish, such as mackerel, herring, and sardines, contain lots of the healthy kind of fat called omega-3. They are also a very good source of vitamins A and D.

Many people believe that omega-3 fatty acids can benefit people's hearts and circulation, and that it especially helps those who have had heart attacks and heart disease. Some people claim that it can also beat depression. Some research has even shown that these fatty acids can make you more intelligent. Some manufacturers advertise their fish oil as "brain food"! Whether or not this is true, we should try to eat at least two portions of fish a week, including one portion of oily omega-3-rich fish.

Comparing oily fish		
3.5-oz (100-g) portion	protein in grams	omega-3 fatty acids in grams
anchovy	20.4	1.4
herring	24.5	1.8
mackerel	25.4	2.2
sardine	20.0	1.7
tuna	25.0	1.6

Labels will tell you whether fish is farmed or caught. If the fish was caught, it will tell you where. China catches by far the most fish and is also the largest exporter. Japan imports the most.

The two fish most often caught are anchovy and pollock, and both live in Pacific waters. The blue whiting lives in the eastern Atlantic, and tuna can cross oceans or even move from one ocean to another.

The world's biggest fishers

total catch in millions of tons per year		exports in millions of U.S. $		imports in millions of U.S. $	
China	18.5	China	5.2	Japan	12.4
Peru	6.7	Thailand	0.9	U.S.A.	11.7
U.S.A.	5.4	Norway	3.6	Spain	4.9
Indonesia	5.2	U.S.A.	3.4	France	3.8
Japan	5.1	Canada	3.3	Italy	3.6
India	4.1	Denmark	3.2	Germany	2.6
Chile	4.0	Spain	2.2	UK	2.5
Russia	3.6	Vietnam	2.2	China	2.4
Thailand	3.1	Netherlands	2.2	Denmark	2.1
Norway	2.9	Chile	2.1	South Korea	1.9

OVERFISHING

In many regions there are simply too many fishermen catching too many fish. This means that fish populations are in decline. The Atlantic cod, for example, used to be one of the most popular fish to eat in the United States and Europe. However, it has been so heavily overfished that less than half as much is sold today as in 1988. Stocks in some areas, including the North Sea, are so low that some experts believe that cod fishing should be banned altogether. The populations of hake, haddock, and flounder have also fallen dramatically.

The most frequently caught fish species	
in millions of tons per year	
Peruvian anchovy	6.8
Alaska pollock	3.2
blue whiting	2.6
skipjack tuna	2.3
Japanese anchovy	2.3
Atlantic herring	2.2
chub mackerel	2.1
Chilean jack mackerel	1.9
yellowfin tuna	1.7
largehead hairtail	1.7

▲ Fishermen protest in northeast England about European quotas. These limit the amount of fish they are allowed to catch in the North Sea. The quotas are set by the European Union for all its member states.

EXPERTS RECOMMEND COD CATCH BAN

"Scientists have recommended that cod fishing is banned in the seas around Scotland. Experts working for the International Council for the Exploration of the Sea (ICES) said it was the only way that **depleted** cod stocks could recover. [...] They also want to see cuts in catches of North Sea plaice and sole, and restrictions on catching effort for monkfish."

From BBC News at bbcnews.com © bbc.co.uk, October 2005

Modern fishing methods are so effective that there is often a large "by-catch." Unwanted fish are caught in the same nets as the fish that are wanted. Some of this by-catch includes species that are **endangered**. Whales, dolphins, seals, and turtles are often killed as by-catch. According to the environmental group Greenpeace, 100 million sharks are killed each year. They say that tuna fisheries alone catch more than a million sharks. An estimated 300,000 whales and dolphins die each year because they cannot escape when caught accidentally in tuna nets.

CHOOSING ORGANIC

Many people care a great deal about what kind of farm their food comes from. They prefer their food to be produced without the use of **pesticides** or artificial **fertilizers**.

Food items labeled "organic" must come from land that has been farmed naturally for at least two years. However, if food products have only some organic ingredients then the food label must reflect that. **Manure** is widely used as an organic fertilizer. It is constantly available on farms that have livestock. Another approach is to rotate crops from year to year, alternating with plants such as alfalfa. This **leguminous** plant restores **nitrogen** to the soil to make it more fertile.

▲ These rows of raspberry bushes grow on an organic farm near the Cascade Mountains in the northwest of North America.

Agritourism

✔ Agritourism (short for agricultural tourism) helps keep some small farms in business. It is especially useful for small organic farms. Families can, for example, stay at a farm in California and enjoy organic avocados or stay at an Australian farm where the speciality is tropical fruits.

✔ Small dairy farms in places like Wisconsin can be vacation spots. Vacationers can enjoy watching traditional methods of farming and can even help with some work.

FOOD WITHOUT SOIL

How would you feel about eating vegetables that have never touched soil? You probably already have, without even knowing it. The process of growing food plants in sand, gravel, or sawdust is called hydroponics. It is used more and more, but is rarely mentioned on food labels. Nutrient solutions and water help the plants to grow, usually under the protection of a plastic greenhouse.

The system is very successful, but costs a lot. It is good for growing high-quality tomatoes, cucumbers, salad crops, and herbs. Farmers tend huge areas of plastic-covered "fields" (without any soil) where they practice controlled environment agriculture (CEA).

▼ Thirty different kinds of vegetables are grown in this hydroponic greenhouse in Houston, Texas. The growers are checking butterhead lettuce.

AROUND THE WORLD:
What is Made Where, and When

Food production depends on climate. Some plants do best in a mild climate, while others grow better where it is generally hotter or colder. The same is true of farm animals. In the past this meant that particular foods were available in certain parts of the world at certain times. Availability depended on the season.

The world trade network means that today many foods are available all year round. It allows produce to be exported from one part of the world, where it is summertime, to another region, where it is winter.

WORLD OF WHEAT

Wheat is probably the world's most important food crop. It generally grows best in cool climates with moderate rainfall. China is the world's leading producer of wheat, and the United States is the largest exporter (see page 5). Wheat harvests are affected by the weather, but it is usually being harvested somewhere in the world at any given time.

Most wheat is ground into flour. Much of this is used to make bread, as well as cakes, cookies, and breakfast cereals. A special kind of wheat, called durum (meaning "hard"), is used to make pasta. It is grown in dry regions.

Monthly wheat harvests around the world	
January	Chile, New Zealand
February	Chile, Myanmar, New Zealand
March	Egypt, India
April	Egypt, India, Iran, Mexico
May	China, Japan, Spain, U.S.A.
June	China, Greece, Spain, Turkey, U.S.A.
July	Bulgaria, France, Germany, Hungary, Russia, UK, Ukraine, U.S.A
August	Canada, Denmark, Russia, UK, Ukraine, U.S.A.
September	Canada, Russia, Scandinavian countries, Scotland
October	Kazakhstan, Norway, Sweden
November	Argentina, Australia, Brazil, South Africa
December	Argentina, Australia

Wheat is also used for many other foods

✔ *Bulgur*: Cereal food from Turkey made from whole wheat that is partially boiled then dried and cracked

✔ *Couscous*: North African semolina (see below) that is made from crushed durum wheat

✔ *Freekeh*: Roasted green wheat that is popular in Arab countries

✔ *Semolina*: Hard grains left after milling wheat that are used in pastas such as spaghetti and macaroni

✔ *Sprouted wheat*: Salad or cooked vegetable that is popular with vegetarians.

▶ After wheat has been harvested, the grain is loaded onto a truck. It is then taken to a grain elevator.

▼ There are lots of different types of bread. Regional specialities have become popular all over the world.

REFINED VERSUS UNREFINED

Grains of wheat are made up of **kernels**. These contain a **husk** called bran, a soft inner part called endosperm, and an **embryo** called a germ. To make white flour (and white bread), millers remove the bran and germ and grind the endosperm only. This refined flour lacks some of the vitamins and **minerals** present in the bran and germ. Whole-wheat or whole-grain flour is made from the entire kernel, and nutritionists say this is better for you.

21

TRAVELING FRUIT

There are thousands of different apple varieties, but most supermarkets sell just a few. Up to 100 varieties are grown commercially in the United States. In states such as New York, Massachusetts, and California, apple-picking farms are popular destinations for tourists.

These days many apples are labeled with their name and country of origin. Take a look the next time you see an apple. You might be surprised to see that it was imported from somewhere else. The United States imports many apples from Chile, New Zealand, and Canada.

▲ Different kinds of apples are for sale at this market, giving customers a wide choice.

Apple origins

✔ Golden Delicious is now the most widely grown apple in many countries. It first appeared in West Virginia around 1900.

✔ Red Delicious is also very popular. It first appeared in Iowa around the 1870s.

✔ Granny Smith is a shiny green apple that grows well in Australia, Chile, France, and South Africa. But who was Granny Smith? She was an Australian—Maria Anne Smith, of Sydney—who first grew this variety around 1865.

✔ McIntosh is a Canadian variety, discovered around 1811 by John McIntosh in Ontario. There are now more than three million McIntosh trees in North America.

Fruit: The world's biggest producers in millions of tons per year

apples	bananas	lemons/ limes	oranges	papayas
China 22.6	India 18.5	Mexico 2.0	Brazil 20.2	Brazil 1.8
U.S.A. 4.7	Brazil 7.3	India 1.5	U.S.A 12.9	Mexico 1.1
Poland 2.8	China 6.6	Iran 1.2	Mexico 4.4	Nigeria 0.9
France 2.6	Ecuador 6.5	Spain 1.2	India 3.4	India 0.8
Iran 2.6	Philippines 6.1	Argentina 1.1	Spain 3.2	Indonesia 0.8

Bananas are a very popular fruit. The main production regions for bananas are African, Caribbean, and Pacific countries, such as Cameroon and St. Lucia, as well as countries in Central and South America. Many Caribbean bananas are produced on small farms, usually owned by local family farmers. In Central and South America, many farms are owned by large **corporations**. They produce what are often called "dollar bananas" because many of the companies are U.S. owned.

Bananas first began to be imported to the United States in the 1870s. They were the first tropical fruit that was available year round to Americans, and they quickly became very popular. Today the United States is the world's largest importer of bananas with most coming from Ecuador, Costa Rica, and Guatemala.

◀ This man loads bananas at a port in Ecuador, South America. Ecuador is the world's largest exporter of bananas.

23

FROM CHINA TO THE WORLD

Tea is a very important drink in many parts of the world. According to legend, a Chinese emperor first drank tea more than 4,700 years ago. Early in the 1600s, Dutch trading ships carried tea from east Asia to Europe. Today China still produces a great deal of tea. Tea plants grow well in warm, wet tropical regions and especially in high, hilly areas. There are three main types of tea:

- Green tea is made from leaves that are dried immediately after picking
- Oolong tea is partially **fermented**
- Black tea is allowed to ferment before being dried.

Other varieties of loose tea or teabags include names such as orange pekoe, Earl Grey, and souchong. Most brands label their teas according to where they come from—Chinese, Indian, Sri Lankan, Kenyan, and so on.

The world's leading tea producers, importers, and drinkers		
tea produced in millions of tons per year	**tea imported in millions of tons per year**	**tea consumed in pounds (kilograms) per person**
India 1.0	Russia 0.2	UK 5.1 (2.3)
China 0.9	UK 0.2	Ireland 3.3 (1.5)
Sri Lanka 0.3	Pakistan 0.1	New Zealand 2.2 (1.0)
Kenya 0.3	U.S.A. 0.1	Japan 2.0 (0.9)

▼ These women pick tea at a plantation in the southern Indian state of Kerala. There, tea plants grow on hillsides up to 5,900 feet (1,800 m) above sea level.

ETHIOPIAN ORIGINS OF COFFEE

It is said that coffee was discovered in ancient Ethiopia. Goatherds noticed that their flocks would not sleep after feeding on coffee berries. As a drink coffee reached Arabia in the 1200s and Europe 300 years later. Coffee was first grown in Brazil in the early 1700s.

Coffee plants grow well in relatively cool climates in the tropics. Today Brazil produces by far the most coffee. Many shops and restaurants label their coffee according to its origin.

▲ Coffee beans are left to dry in the sun in the Kaffa region of Ethiopia. This country, where coffee was first discovered, is still Africa's largest producer.

The world's leading coffee producers, importers, and drinkers

coffee produced in millions of tons per year	coffee imported in millions of tons per year	coffee consumed in pounds (kilograms) per person
Brazil 2.8	U.S.A. 1.3	Norway 23.6 (10.7)
Vietnam 0.9	Germany 1.0	Finland 22.3 (10.1)
Indonesia 0.8	Italy 0.4	Denmark 21.4 (9.7)
Colombia 0.8	Japan 0.4	Sweden 17.2 (7.8)

DAIRY PRODUCTS

Milk produced on dairy farms is turned into many other foods, called dairy products. These include butter, cheese, and yogurt. In most industrialized countries, cows are raised to produce milk, and many different kinds of cheese are made from their milk. But in some parts of the world, the milk of goats, sheep, buffaloes, and even horses is used to make cheese. In northern Scandinavia, herders use reindeer milk, and in Tibet people turn yaks' milk into butter and cheese.

The leading producers of milk

Animal	Country
buffalo	India, Pakistan, China, Egypt, Nepal
camel	Somalia, Saudi Arabia, Sudan, Mali, United Arab Emirates
cow	U.S.A., India, Russia, Germany, France
goat	India, Bangladesh, Sudan, Pakistan, France
sheep	China, Italy, Turkey, Greece, Syria

TRADITIONAL CHEESES

Cheese is traditionally made in different ways in various countries. The different kinds are usually named according to their origin. Buyers might not notice that their favorite cheese is not actually made in the country they expect. One of the world's most popular cheeses is cheddar, which is a smooth, hard cheese made from cow's milk. It originated around 800 years ago in the English village of the same name.

Most of the world's cheddar is now produced in other countries, including Australia, Canada, Ireland, New Zealand, South Africa, Sweden, and the United States. Producers are allowed to call their cheese cheddar, which now refers more to the kind of cheese rather than the place of origin.

Some cheese names are protected. For example, Roquefort must be made from sheep's milk treated with a special mold and matured in caves near the village of Roquefort, in southern France. The mold makes blue streaks in the cheese and gives it a special flavor.

Many other cheese-making villages, regions, and countries campaign to have the same protection for their names.

▲ Roquefort cheese is checked carefully.
The sheep's milk takes at least three
months to mature in special caves.

GREECE WINS FIGHT TO USE THE WORD "FETA"

The European Court of Justice has ruled that only cheese made in certain areas of Greece may use the name "feta." Feta claims a 6,000-year history in Greece. This ruling does not directly affect the United States, however. The United States does not produce sheep's milk. This means it cannot produce feta cheese, since feta is supposed to be made from sheep's milk. Various forms of feta cheese are made in the United States, though, usually from cows' milk.

In the news, October 2005

Where some famous cheeses originally came from

- ✔ Brie: Meaux, France
- ✔ Edam: Edam, Netherlands
- ✔ Emmental: Emme Valley, Switzerland
- ✔ Parmesan: Parma, Italy
- ✔ Stilton: Stilton, England

VEGETABLE GROUPS

Vegetables are important, **nutritious** foods that come from different parts of edible plants. We can divide them into eight different groups, from bulbs and roots underground to stems and leaves above it.

Wild plants were very important to prehistoric people who hunted and gathered their food. Some of the wild varieties were planted and grown by the earliest farming communities. Experts have tried to figure out where the vegetables that we eat today first grew.

Vegetables and their wild origins		
vegetable group	**examples and probable origins**	
bulb	garlic, central Asia	leek, east Mediterranean
flower buds	broccoli, Italy	cauliflower, east Mediterranean
fruit	eggplant, India	cucumber, India
leaves	cabbage, north Europe	spinach, Iran
roots	carrot, Afghanistan	turnip, north Europe
seeds*	pea, west Asia	scarlet runner bean, Mexico
stems	asparagus, east Europe	kohlrabi (a cabbage), France
tubers	potato, Peru	Jerusalem artichoke, North America

* For more on seeds, see page 30.

▼ Long rows of spinach grow on this large farm in Colorado.

The world's biggest vegetable producers in millions of tons per year

asparagus	eggplant	cabbage	lettuce	spinach
China 6.4	China 18.2	China 35.3	China 11.6	China 11.9
Peru 0.2	India 9.0	India 6.6	U.S.A. 4.8	U.S.A. 0.4
U.S.A. 0.1	Turkey 1.1	Russia 5.0	Spain 1.1	Japan 0.3
Mexico 0.08	Egypt 0.8	South Korea 3.1	Italy 1.0	Turkey 0.2
Germany 0.07	Iraq 0.4	U.S.A. 2.8	India 0.9	France 0.1

▲ These men sell vegetables at a market in southern India. Eggplant originated in India, where it is still widely grown.

China dominates the modern production of vegetables. The examples above show how much more China produces than other countries (for potatoes, see page 9). There are more than 200 million Chinese farming families, and since 1990 their food production has nearly doubled.

China has the biggest population of all the world's countries, with more than 1,300 million people—more than one-fifth of the world's total. This means that most Chinese produce is needed at home. You will not find a lot of Chinese produce in your supermarket. The biggest exporters of the vegetables listed on the chart above are Peru for asparagus, Spain for eggplant and lettuce, and the United States for cabbage and spinach.

WHAT IS A NUT ... A SEED ... A PULSE?

The names of these important foodstuffs are confusing. This is mainly because they are all really seeds. A nut is actually a tree fruit with a hard outer shell around an edible kernel (sometimes called a seed). Hazelnuts and walnuts are examples of nuts. Seeds are the embryo and food supply of new plants, such as pumpkins or sunflowers. Pulses are edible seeds from a pod, such as peas, beans, and lentils, which are also classed as vegetables. Nuts, seeds, and pulses are all good sources of protein, **fiber**, vitamins, and minerals.

To which food group do peanuts belong?

We call them nuts, but peanuts are really seeds (and they belong to the family of pulses!). They are also called groundnuts because they grow underground. The plant's flowers thrust stems into the ground, where the pods develop. Each pod usually contains two seeds. People usually call the pods shells and the seeds nuts.

MACADAMIA NUTS

The early Aboriginal peoples of Australia were no doubt eating the nuts of the macadamia tree thousands of years ago. In the 1800s two botanists studied the tree, and one of them named it after his friend, a chemist named John Macadam (1827–1865). Commercial orchards started producing nuts in the 1880s, when the tree was also introduced to Hawaii.

► Nuts are carried by a conveyor belt at a macadamia orchard in Hawaii.

Origin of some nuts and today's biggest producers

nut	origin	biggest producers
almond	southwest Asia	U.S.A., Syria, Iran
cashew	Central America	Vietnam, India, Brazil
hazelnut	southern Europe	Turkey, Italy, U.S.A.
macadamia	Australia	Australia, U.S.A. (Hawaii), Malawi
peanut	Peru	China, India, Nigeria
pistachio	southwest Asia	Iran, U.S.A., Turkey
walnut	west Asia	China, U.S.A., Iran

Seedy facts

Pumpkin seeds:

✔ Come from the pumpkin plant, which probably originated in North America

✔ Are produced the most in China, India, and Ukraine

✔ Are rich in iron, zinc, and phosphorus

✔ Can be eaten raw or cooked.

Sesame seeds:

✔ Come from a herb that grew originally in Africa and India

✔ Are used to flavor bread and crackers

✔ Are produced the most in India, China, and Myanmar

✔ Give a straw-colored oil, used in cooking

✔ Are ground into a paste called tahini that is used in hummus

✔ Are a good source of calcium, iron, and **niacin.**

▲ Pumpkin seeds have a variety of uses.

Sunflower seeds:

✔ Come from sunflowers, which belong to the daisy family and originated in North America

✔ Are produced the most in Russia, Ukraine, and Argentina

✔ Are rich in potassium, phosphorus, iron, and calcium

✔ Produce a very popular vegetable oil.

PACKED AND TRANSPORTED:
How Does the Food Get to You

The food you eat may have traveled a long way from where it was produced to where you bought it. Good packaging makes long-distance travel possible by making foods easy to handle for carriers and retailers. The packaging also protects foodstuffs from damage and protects them against dirt, harmful **bacteria**, and other dangerous substances.

Canning is a traditional method of packing food into a can to preserve it. The first canned tomatoes were produced in Pennsylvania around 1850, and canned peas followed a few years later. California peaches were sold in cans from the 1860s.

Raw food is prepared before canning. It is usually cleaned, peeled, cut, and sliced. It is then poured into cans automatically on a production line. The food is usually topped off with water, **brine**, sauce, or syrup, leaving a space of about 0.2 inches (6 millimeters). Some of the air in this space is removed, creating a partial **vacuum**. This makes it more difficult for bacteria to grow.

Next, the can is sealed so that it is airtight. Some metal lids have a ring pull so that you do not have to use a can opener. Then, the can is heated, killing any bacteria that might otherwise spoil the food. Finally, the can is cooled by cold water or air.

Canning facts

- ✔ Most food cans are made from tinplate (a sheet steel coated with tin). Some are made from aluminum.
- ✔ Lacquers and enamels are applied to the metal, depending on the intended contents.
- ✔ Over 32 billion food cans are used in the United States every year.
- ✔ Canned food can be stored at room temperature and has a very long shelf life.
- ✔ Can labels give both a total weight and a drained weight. A can of chickpeas in water with a total weight of 14.4 ounces (410 grams) actually weighs 16.9 ounces (480 grams). It consists of 8.4 ounces (240 grams) of chickpeas, 5.9 ounces (170 grams) of water, and 2.5 ounces (70 grams) for the can.

▲ Picked peaches are taken away from an orchard.

QUICK COOLING

Some vegetables are cooled as soon as they are picked. They are then packed in cartons and kept cool for the trip to the market or supermarket. Vacuum cooling is much faster than ordinary cooling in a refrigerator. Picked vegetables are put into a special cooler, which allows water vapor to rise and the vegetables to cool. If they leave the field at 79 °F (26 °C), the vegetables can be cooled down to about 34 °F (1 °C) within 25 minutes.

▶ These new cans are on the production line, ready to be filled with food.

OFF TO MARKET

Since fresh foods quickly go bad, they must be transported to markets and stores as rapidly as possible. Most foods are carried by road in refrigerated trucks or by rail in refrigerated train cars. For longer distances, river barges or ocean-going ships are used. Some expensive, highly **perishable** foods are flown in cargo aircraft.

▼ Cartons of fish are loaded into a refrigerated truck at a port in Norway.

The distance food travels from where it is grown to where it is consumed can be calculated in so-called "food miles." As national and international trade has increased, the distances covered by food-carrying vehicles have also gone up. During the 21st century, they will increase at an even faster rate unless more efforts are made to buy local produce.

U.S. researchers at Iowa State University found that fruits and vegetables traveled to the state's stores and supermarkets from all over the United States. This is despite the fact that Iowa has about 60,000 farms of its own. The produce that came from local farmers and suppliers traveled an average of 56 miles (90 kilometers), about one-fifth of the width of the state. But the food that came from the rest of the United States traveled 1,490 miles (2,400 kilometers) on average. Out-of-state broccoli traveled more than 90 times farther than in-state broccoli.

In Europe German experts studied strawberry-flavored yogurt on sale in Stuttgart. They found that the strawberries had been imported from Poland (which supplies 8 percent of Germany's imported strawberries, much less than the 64 percent from farther-away Spain). The milk was from southern Germany, but the yogurt cultures came from the north of the country. The sugar in the yogurt was from east German beet, and the corn and wheat flour came from the Netherlands. Researchers calculated that yogurt arriving at the production company's distribution center had traveled an average of more than 621 miles (1,000 kilometers).

▼ Barges carry fruits and vegetables to a store in Venice, Italy, where boats are the main form of transportation.

Imports closer to home

For many years the United States was a major exporter of apples and apple juice to the Asian market. This required many miles of fuel to be used, and as a result it caused a lot of pollution. In recent years China has begun to surpass the United States as the major supplier of apples and apple juice to many parts of Asia, including southeast Asia. This cuts down on travel time and pollution.

BUYING FOOD DIRECT

Many food producers now sell direct to their customers. Buyers place their order by phone, email, or on the supplier's website, and the food is delivered to their door. The advantage of buying direct is that suppliers often tell you in their literature exactly where the food comes from, how it was produced, and how it will get to you.

Many companies sell organic food, which they advertise as "fresh from the grower." Some offer benefits that are very useful to the environment. For example, they:

- Reuse cardboard or wooden delivery boxes
- Use **biodegradable** plastic for box covers
- Run vans on **biofuel**
- Turn leftover vegetables into compost
- Import some produce by ship, but never by air (because aircraft make much more pollution).

MAP PACKAGING

Producers are constantly looking for new forms of packaging. They want to protect food and prolong shelf life. One new form is called modified-atmosphere packaging (MAP). As food is wrapped in plastic, the amounts of oxygen, carbon dioxide, and other gases are changed inside the package. This "modified atmosphere" (changed air) stops bacteria from growing. MAP is used for packing meat, bread, fruits, and vegetables.

A common use of MAP is for bags of lettuce. But some studies have shown that this reduces the nutritional value of the lettuce. The process removes some vitamins and **antioxidants**. So the lettuce looks very fresh and appetizing in the supermarket, but it may not be or taste as good as it looks. Also, the lettuce turns brown very quickly after the hi-tech package is opened.

SALAD DAYS QUESTIONED

"Prepacked salad leaves may not be as nutritious as they look. Research suggests a processing technique used to prolong shelf-life may remove vital nutrients. Tests showed salad bags did not boost vitamin C levels in the body like fresh lettuce. Some nutritionists say this should not deter people from eating prepacked salad leaves, since they contain other goodness, such as fiber."

From BBC News at bbcnews.com © bbc.co.uk, March 18, 2003

▲ This lobster's claws are tied so that it will not pinch the cook. Many cooks drop a live lobster into a pot of boiling water to kill and then cook it. They claim the animal feels no pain. Others consider this to be cruel.

Live lobster to your door

✔ Several companies in Maine specialize in selling live lobsters. They catch the animals in lobster pots off the coast and store them in cooled seawater tanks. This means they always have some available.

✔ When you order a lobster from their website, they pack it with a cold pack into an insulated cardboard container. Then it is sent by refrigerated truck either directly to you or to the nearest airport and then on to you. They deliver throughout the United States with next-day service.

SUPERMARKETS:
Where Most People Buy Their Food

Do you and your family buy most of your food in a local supermarket? That is what most people in the wealthier, industrialized countries of the world do. Supermarkets carry a wide range of all the major foods and sell them at good prices. Many families go shopping once a week and get everything they need in one store.

Your grandparents may have shopped at small grocery stores for food and other household goods. They went to a produce market for fresh fruits and vegetables, to the butcher for meat, and to a seafood market for fish and seafood. But times have changed for small stores, which struggle to compete with supermarkets. Most Americans no longer, or rarely, visit these smaller stores.

▼ Shoppers check out the canned soup and other produce in a 1950s supermarket.

Big business

✔ In the United States, 85 percent of perishable foods are sold in supermarkets.

✔ In recent years a new trend has developed as "mega-stores", such as Wal-Mart®, have expanded their merchandise to include large selections of groceries. This is beginning to pose a challenge to established supermarket chains.

The first supermarkets were opened in the United States in the 1930s. They sold only food and operated under the slogan "Pile it high, sell it low"—in other words, have lots of foods for shoppers to choose from and sell them at low prices. Most foods were sold loose (without packaging) and were displayed in cardboard boxes and shipping containers.

By the 1950s supermarkets had become the main outlets for food in the United States. During the second half of the 20th century, they gradually added new goods to sell in addition to food.

Today many supermarkets sell cooking utensils, cleaning products, greetings cards, and many other items. They even have their own banks, discount cards, and other financial incentives to encourage you to spend money with them.

Before the 1920s products were brought to the customer by a store assistant who stood on one side of a counter. Customers stood on the other side and asked for what they wanted. Then self-service shopping helped supermarkets cut costs. Today many supermarkets cut costs by using self-service checkout machines. Four or five machines can then be supervised by one assistant.

Most experts predict that supermarkets will continue to grow bigger and gain a larger share of the food market. In the future there may be no small food stores left at all. Do you think that would be a good thing?

PURCHASING POWER

Imagine you are a small farmer. If a big supermarket chain offers you a guaranteed amount of money for most of your produce for the foreseeable future, what would you do? You might be able to get a higher price for your produce locally, but that means more deliveries and less certainty of selling all your produce. **Environmentalists** say that this pressure on farmers to sell to the big supermarkets means that some supermarkets are telling farmers what to grow. If they cannot get what they want locally, the supermarkets simply buy from abroad.

SUPERMARKET PRICES

Supermarkets compete with each other to sell food at low prices. Often they try to convince shoppers that their prices are best by selling items at a very low profit or even below cost. These bargains are attractive to customers and encourage them to buy from that store.

The lowest prices are often given to "known price items," such as bread or milk. The idea is that people tend to know the usual price of these foods and so recognize a bargain. We base our idea of value on a few important foods. Selling food at less than cost is not allowed in some countries, in order to protect small store owners who cannot compete.

▼ Supermarkets tempt their customers with special offers, hoping that they will spend more money.

Very often you will find bread and other essential foods at the back of the supermarket. They are placed there so that you have to pass lots of other tempting items on your way. Like all products, foods sell well in shelf positions known as "hot spots." Foods positioned at eye level sell best ("eye level is buy level"), along with those in the middle of an aisle or at the end of a block of shelves.

Getting lost!

In order to influence our decisions, supermarkets put a lot of thought into where they place different foods. They also change the layout of stores often so that regular customers see different products on their usual route.

WHERE DOES THE PACKAGING GO?

Supermarkets demand that suppliers provide food items that are well wrapped and packaged. This may help keep certain foods in good condition, but it is also popular with sellers because it makes food items look attractive. Do you think you might be influenced in your choice of breakfast cereal, for example, by the design of the box? If you are not, you are probably the exception.

The problem is that this form of marketing causes a huge amount of waste packaging. A lot of the cardboard and other material can be recycled. In some countries, such as Germany, supermarkets encourage customers to unwrap their goods after passing the checkout and leave the packaging at the store. The packaging can then be sent for recycling.

▼ Cardboard boxes are gathered at a supermarket, ready to be collected for recycling.

CONVENIENCE FOOD:
Eating for Ease and Speed

When eating at home, many people prefer meals that can be prepared quickly and easily. When eating out, they like their food to be delivered almost at once or within a few minutes.

The idea of fast-food restaurants started 50 years ago in the United States. Fast-food chains have since spread all around the world. The most popular serve hamburgers, pizza, or fried chicken, and most meals come with French fries.

It is important that you make careful choices at these types of restaurants. Young people should consider a children's meal rather than a large value meal. Think about the portion-size that you need. Fast-food companies have recently started printing facts about nutritional values on menus and packaging. This is because some companies are criticized by people who claim that their food is poor quality—too fatty, too salty, or full of artificial flavors and colors.

► Western-style fast food is served on this busy street in a shopping district of Shanghai, in China.

Large fast-food chains also run websites giving information about the ingredients they use and their health value. The charts on these websites allow you to compare the calories, fat, and more for different meal options. Unfortunately these informative sites and leaflets do not usually say much about the origin of their foods. In the United States, one of the largest fast-food companies says that the beef in its burgers is "100% pure USDA inspected beef" (the USDA is the U.S. Department of Agriculture), but the origins are not given.

▶ Ready-to-eat food is popular all over the world. This woman is preparing food at a stall in a market in Vietnam.

Hoki

✔ Hoki, a kind of fish also known as the blue grenadier, was once thought of as an inferior species. Today it has become one of the most widely used in fast-food restaurants in the United States and elsewhere.

✔ Most hoki, which is widespread in New Zealand, is exported to the United States, Europe, Japan, and Australia. The total catch each year is set at a limit, so that stocks of the fish do not go down too much.

✔ In some parts of the world, fast-food restaurants use North Atlantic pollock or cod, as well as hoki.

PIZZA FROM NAPLES?

No one is certain of the exact history of pizza, but it was probably first made in Naples, in southern Italy. The story goes that it was a popular dish among the poor people of Naples during the 1700s. It became better known after King Umberto I visited Naples with his queen, Margherita of Savoy, in 1889. The queen enjoyed a taste of pizza, and its fame soon spread.

WOW!

Americans love pizza! Every second about 350 slices of pizza are eaten in the United States. Every year about three billion pizzas are sold across the country. One poll shows that 94 percent of Americans eat pizza.

Italian emigrants took recipes with them to the United States, where pizza also became very popular. The pizza *Margherita*, made with mozzarella cheese, tomatoes, and basil, was named after the queen. The ingredients represented the three stripes of the Italian flag: green, white, and red.

In pizza restaurants today, it is difficult to tell where all the ingredients come from. Even the pizza crust is a complicated food item. One famous pizza chain lists its ingredients for pan pizza as wheat flour, ascorbic acid, water, frozen yeast, salt, soy oil, whey powder, panadan (datem), cf05, monoglyceride, holzyme 450 (fungal alpha amylase complex), emulsifiers, monoglyceride, and fatty acid esters of glycerides (calcium carbonate).

MAKING GOOD FAST-FOOD CHOICES

Not all fast food is a poor choice. But it is important to balance it out by choosing a wide variety of foods. This will help you have a balanced, healthy diet. Remember to eat lots of fruits and vegetables, whole-grain versions of starchy foods when you can, and small quantities of fat, salt, and sugar.

In a fast-food restaurant you should choose:

✔ Food that is grilled or baked rather than fried
✔ A side salad with low-fat dressing or a baked potato rather than French fries
✔ Mustard or ketchup instead of mayonnaise or "special sauce"
✔ Water or juice, and go easy on the soda
✔ Fruit and yogurt instead of sweet desserts.

Pizza varieties and Italian cities

✔ Pizza *Fiorentina* (spinach, Parmesan cheese, and egg): from Florence

✔ *Napoletana* (tomatoes, mozzarella cheese, anchovies, and capers): from Naples

✔ *Parmense* (asparagus, ham, and Parmesan cheese): from Parma

✔ *Romana* (tomatoes, mozzarella cheese, Pecorino cheese, and anchovies): from Rome

✔ *Siciliana* (artichoke hearts, anchovies, and ham): from Sicily

✔ *Veneziana* (onions, capers, olives, raisins, and pine nuts): from Venice

▼ Pizza is a popular choice for a quick, easy meal.

LOCAL FOOD:
Help Limit the Food Miles

Would you and your family like to help keep down the food miles? If so buy food produced locally. Local produce has become more popular in recent years, even in large cities. Shoppers buy from farmers' markets, where growers and producers from the nearby region sell their food in person direct to the public.

Registered farmers' markets in New York City and elsewhere in the world are checked to see that the produce is of high quality. Many sell organic produce. This is an advantage, because much of the organic food available in large supermarkets travels a long distance to the store, increasing food miles.

There are 54 farmers' markets in New York City, and 23 of them are open all year round. The others are seasonal. They are there so that 175 farmers can sell their fruits, vegetables, fish, meat, eggs, dairy, honey, maple syrup, plants, and other foods. The oldest and biggest market, which first opened in 1976, is in Union Square. It is open four days a week every week and has become an important part of the local community. The farmers also supply produce to many local restaurants.

▶ Pumpkins are sold at Union Square farmers' market in New York.

VEGETABLES OF THE WORLD

Farmers' markets in North America and Europe sell vegetables, such as beans, broccoli, cabbage, carrots, lettuce, onions, potatoes, spinach, and tomatoes. Markets in other parts of the world might sell quite different vegetables. In a small market in Kenya, Africa, many different vegetables might be on sale, such as amaranth, black nightshade, cowpeas, jute plant (or nalta jute), kale, pigweed, spider flower (or spiderwisp), and sunn hemp. Many of these plants also grow elsewhere, but they are rarely used as food in other parts of the world.

▼ Beans, seeds, and pulses form just part of the produce in this colorful market in Kenya.

Micro-livestock

Would you like to try eating insects? If so, you might like the markets in the following countries, where edible insects are sold. Some are very nutritious. Gram for gram, termites have twice as much protein as beef. But do not ever eat any insects at home. They might be poisonous!

✔ Mexico: Grasshoppers (for frying), agave worms

✔ Colombia: Termites, palm grubs, ants (used as a spread on toast)

✔ Philippines: Junebugs, mole crickets, dragonfly larvae

✔ Papua New Guinea: Sago grubs (for boiling or roasting), stick insects

IDEAS FOR HEALTHY EATING

People eat nutritious food all over the world. This does more than keep people healthy—it also adds pleasure to their lives. Here are some favorite healthy dishes from the world's continents.

AUSTRALIA

- Beef is popular in Australia, along with lamb, pork, and poultry. Meat is often grilled on a barbecue and served with potatoes and vegetables.
- In New Zealand, lamb is a favorite, served with *kumara* (sweet potatoes) and soup made with *toheroa*, a native green clam
- Pacific islanders have lived for centuries on seafood. They cook crabs, lobsters, shrimps, and fish, along with a root vegetable called *taro*.

EUROPE

Dishes from France and Italy are popular all over the world, for example:
- French *ratatouille*, which is onions, tomatoes, peppers, zucchini, and eggplant, stewed in olive oil
- Italian *spaghetti alle vongole*, which is strings of pasta with clams.

ASIA

In China rice is generally served with every meal, such as:
- Stir-fried crispy seaweed and spring rolls
- Pork *chow mein*, which is thinly sliced pork fillets with peppers, spring onions, bean sprouts, and noodles stir-fried with sesame oil
- Chicken and noodle soup with bamboo shoots, grated ginger, and mushrooms.

In India foods are highly seasoned with spices:
- *Biriani pilau* is flavored rice with turmeric, cilantro, green chili, and cumin, cooked with boned lamb, chicken, or fish
- *Parathas* is Indian bread stuffed with spiced potato purée and minced onion or ground meat and lentils
- *Aloo saag* is made of spinach, potatoes, and Indian spices.

Why "hamburger"?

German immigrants took steak from Hamburg to the United States in the 1800s. The first "hamburgers" (Hamburg steak in a bun) were sold at the St. Louis World Fair in 1904.

AFRICA

- A favorite dish in northern Africa is couscous (see page 21). A stew of meat, fish, and vegetables is cooked in the lower part of a stockpot and the couscous is steamed in the upper part.
- Meat and fish stews are also cooked in a *tagine*. This is a shallow dish with a conical lid that is ideal for long, slow simmering.
- Moroccan *briouats* and Algerian *boureks* are triangular pieces of dough filled with chicken and spinach
- In South Africa *potjie kos* is very popular. A *potjie* is a heavy, three-legged pot that is used on an open fire. Any type of meat and mixture of vegetables is slowly stewed in it.

NORTH AMERICA

Some well-known specialities are:

- New England clam chowder, which is a soup with clams, potatoes, and onions cooked in milk and cream
- Boston baked beans, which is dried navy beans with salt pork, dark brown sugar, and mustard baked in a casserole for four to five hours
- Mexican tortillas, which are flat, thin corn or wheat flour pancakes with fillings such as shredded chicken, chilis, and tomatoes.

SOUTH AMERICA

Some favorite dishes are:

- Brazilian *feijoada*, which is a meat stew with black beans and rice
- Colombian *ajiaco* soup, which has potatoes, chicken, corn, and cassava (the root of a plant).

▲ Muslim men eat a meal together in Morocco, North Africa.

RECIPES

DHAL

As an ingredient in Indian food, "dhal" means split pulses. They can be split garbanzo beans, lentils, or beans. "Dhal" also means a spicy stew made from these pulses. It is eaten with bread, rice, and curried vegetables. This recipe, which comes from Bengal, uses red lentils, which are high in vitamin B6. The golden turmeric powder comes from the root of a south Asian plant.

Ingredients:
3 cups red lentils
3 cups water
3 tablespoons vegetable oil
2 small onions, finely chopped
2 garlic cloves, finely chopped
$1/2$ fresh green chili, seeded
    and finely chopped
$1/2$ teaspoon ground turmeric
2 dried red chilis, crushed
1 teaspoon ground cilantro
$1/2$ teaspoon ground cumin
$1/2$–1 teaspoon salt
3 teaspoons lemon juice
3 tablespoons fresh cilantro,
    chopped

▲ These ingredients make a delicious dahl dish.

Method:
Wash the lentils and put them in a medium-sized pan. Add the water and bring to a boil. Add the turmeric, cover, and simmer for 15 to 20 minutes, or until the lentils are very soft. Mash the lentils with a fork and mix in the salt. Heat the oil in a small frying pan and gently cook the onion, without browning, for about 8 minutes. Add the garlic and green chili and cook for another 3 minutes. Combine the ground cilantro, cumin, crushed red chili, and lemon juice in a small bowl. Add 1 teaspoon of water and mix to a paste. Stir the paste into the onion mixture and fry for 2 to 3 minutes. Pour over the lentils in the pan and mix well. Return to the heat, cover, and simmer for 10 minutes. Stir once or twice to make sure the mixture does not stick to the bottom. The dhal should be like a thick stew. If it is too dry, add a little more water. Sprinkle with chopped cilantro and serve hot. Serves 4 to 6 people.

▲ This fruit salad will give you a real vitamin boost.

EXOTIC FRUIT SALAD

You can use whichever fruits are in season and available in your local market. Guavas have lots of vitamin C.

Ingredients:

1 large mango
1 papaya
1 guava
1 pineapple
2 bananas
1/2 melon

2 passion fruits
juice and grated rind of 1 lime
juice of 1 orange
1 tablespoon sesame seeds
2 kiwi fruits, peeled and sliced

Method:

Peel and cut the mango, papaya, guava, pineapple, bananas, and melon into small pieces and put into a large bowl. Cut the passion fruits in half and scoop out the seeds with a teaspoon. Add them to the bowl. Mix in the juice and rind of the lime as well as the orange juice. Sprinkle with sesame seeds and decorate with kiwi slices. Serve with yogurt. Serves 4 to 6 people.

GLOSSARY

agent person who organizes things, such as buying and selling, for others

antioxidant substance that stops certain chemical reactions from causing food to decay

bacteria (plural of bacterium) single-celled microscopic organisms

battery cages cages female chickens (hens) are kept in at intensive factory farms

biodegradable made of a substance that can be broken down by bacteria or in other natural ways. It therefore does not cause pollution.

biofuel fuel produced from plant or animal matter, such as sugarcane or vegetable oil

brine salt water

cereal grain seed from cereal plants, such as corn, wheat, or rice

corporation large company or group of companies

crop plants grown for food

cured made to last longer by smoking, drying, or salting

deplete reduce or use up

embryo part of a seed that grows into a new plant

endangered in danger of dying out

environmentalist person who cares about and acts to protect nature

export sell goods to another country and send them there. The goods are called exports.

factory ship large fishing vessel that can freeze its own catch on board

ferment break down with a substance, such as yeast or bacteria

fertilizer chemical or natural substance added to soil to provide plants with nutrients that help them grow

fiber substance in plants that help people digest the food they have eaten

husk outer covering of some grains and nuts

import buy goods from another country. The goods are called imports.

intensive factory farming using technology to produce as much food as possible

kernel grain of a cereal plant that contains a seed and husk

leguminous belonging to a family of plants that have seeds in pods, such as peas

manure animal dung used as fertilizer

mineral solid chemical substance that occurs naturally in the soil. To be healthy we need certain minerals in small quantities.

niacin type of vitamin B

nitrogen gas that makes up a large part of air

nutrient substance in food that provides nourishment (helping us grow and be healthy)

nutritious helping growth and health

omega-3 type of unsaturated fatty acid mainly found in oily fish and in other foods, such as milk

perishable likely to decay and go bad quickly

pesticide chemical substance used to destroy pests, especially insects

protein natural substance made up of amino acids that acts as a nutrient in food

sorghum cereal plant grown for its grain

surplus more of something than needed

vacuum space from which all air has been removed

vitamin one of a group of substances we need to be healthy

world trade network system that links traders across the world, allowing them to buy from and sell to each other

FINDING OUT MORE

GROWING YOUR OWN FOOD

Growing your own food is the easiest way you can get local food. You will cause zero food miles! If you have a garden or backyard, or even some pots or tubs, you could try growing herbs or vegetables. There may also be public areas near you where you can share a plot. You will find lots of books on the subject in your local library or bookstore. You might also find tips and ideas at a garden center where you can buy seeds.

VISIT A FARM

A real working farm will give you an idea of how food is produced on a small scale. Do not just turn up at a farm and hope for a good reception. Look on the Internet for a list of working farms that are near you. Try contacting your state Department of Agriculture or your tourism board.

LOOK CLOSELY AT LABELS

If you live in or near a big town or city, look for stores, mini-markets, or delicatessens that sell food from different cultures. Look closely at the labels to see where the food comes from. You might like to try a different version of a food that you like.

BOOKS

Body Needs series: Titles include *Carbohydrates for a Healthy Body, Fats for a Healthy Body, Proteins for a Healthy Body, Vitamins and Minerals for a Healthy Body,* and *Water and Fiber for a Healthy Body.* Chicago: Heinemann Library, 2003. This series looks at what the human body needs to function healthily.

Buller, Laura. *Food.* New York: Dorling Kindersley, 2005.

Davidson, Alan. *Penguin Companion to Food.* New York: Penguin, 2002.

Mason, Paul. *Planet Under Pressure: Food.* Chicago: Heinemann Library, 2006.

Morgan, Sally. *Science at the Edge: Genetic Modification of Foods.* Chicago: Heinemann Library, 2002. Learn more about genetically modified foods.

A World of Recipes series: Titles include *Indonesia, Egypt, Spain, Russia, Vietnam,* and *Vegetarian Recipes from Around the World.* Chicago: Heinemann Library, 2003.

WEBSITES

www.usda.gov

This is the site of the U.S. Department of Agriculture (USDA), which is responsible for food and nutrition in the United States.

www.fda.gov

This is the site of the U.S. Food and Drug Administration, an agency of the U.S. Department of Health and Human Services.

www.ams.usda.gov/nop

This section of the USDA website, part of the National Organic Program, offers information on organic food and farming.

www.fao.org

This Food and Agricultural Organization of the United Nations website offers food statistics from around the world.

For more information on Fair Trade, visit these sites:
- International: **www.fairtrade.net**
- United States: **www.transfairusa.org**

For more information on environmental groups, visit these sites:
- Greenpeace: **www.greenpeace.org/usa**
- Friends of the Earth: **www.foei.org**

INDEX